Journal

Settings Christian Publishing, LLC

Calhan, CO

Published 2020
Printed in the United States of America
ISBN: 978-1-7348040-2-7

Cover and Interior designed by Settings Christian Publishing, LLC

www.settingschristian.com

Journal: Vietnam Flower Art

Artwork created by the children of Hope's Promise Vietnam

Hope's Promise

The mission of Hope's Promise is to transform lives through the Christian ministry of adoption and orphan care. When orphaned and vulnerable children are unable to remain in the care of biological relatives due to death, neglect, or abuse, Hope's Promise partners with indigenous Christian leaders and local churches in Kenya, Vietnam, and Nepal to create informal foster families, empowering and equipping parents to provide for the children's physical, emotional, social, and spiritual needs. Learn more at https://www.hopespromise.com/christian-orphan-care

Your purchase of this journal will help Hope's Promise fulfill their mission. Thank you.